Milan.

Milan. It might not p[...] grandeur of Rome or Florence. [...] capital has the energy to draw [...] attractions to keep you there. [...]

The northern city is known for its cocktail of old and new—setting traditional trattorias beside radical design galleries. And the same goes for the people— over an aperitivo in a bar you might find a captain of industry deep in conversation with a mechanic.

And it's the people who shape the feel of the city. In Milan, we spoke to gifted personalities: a creative force setting the global graphic scene alight, a pair of industrial designers, an architect and art-book editor and a food blogger duo. Discover the contro-versial regeneration of the Isola neighbourhood, and read some hot pulp from a local crime writer. It's all about original minds and the creative vibe. Get lost in the sights, sounds and flavours of the city. Get lost in Milan.

In a city known for its centuries-old architecture, Milan is host to an unusually modern building known as the *Torre Velasca*. This 1950s minimalist skyscraper stands at over 100 metres tall and soars above the low skyline of Milan's historic city centre. Set among ancient cathedrals and domes, its concrete exterior, asymmetrical window patterns and mushroom-like shape certainly catch the eye. Sadly, it's a bit trickier to get an inside look—the building is privately-owned and used almost entirely for offices and apartments. The lower floors nevertheless contain a few stores, cafés and exhibits to explore.

Torre Velasca, Centro, torrevelasca.it

Concealed Beauty

Set in an old hidden workshop, the showroom of Antonio Marras reveals the influences of his designs and his passion for art and craftsmanship. Aside from the clothing on display at *Nonostantemarras*, the showroom is an amalgamation of various weathered objects, from those collected on travels around the globe to items from the nearby Navigli flea market. A perfect example are the wooden drawers that house books in the library; Antonio discovered them at a needle factory in Piedmont.

• Nonostantemarras, Tortona, antoniomarras.it

From Design Legends to Rooftop Pools

Forza Milano

Food **Finger Licking Lunch**

The Milanese love a Saturday lunch with friends or family at the *Giannasi 1967*. This location boasts several Italian specialities: lasagna, arancini (sicilian fried rice balls), gnocchi or a creamy Risotto alla Milanese. But the place is famous for its roast chicken: Dorando Giannasi is the owner of the kiosk which originally opened as a poultry shop. In forty years of business, Giannasi has never altered the chicken recipe which aromatises for 24 hours and broils for an additional couple of hours afterward.

• Giannasi 1967, Porta Romana, giannasi1967milano.blogspot.de

Culture | Caves of Creativity

Achille Castiglioni brought us lighting classics like the table lamp Gibigiana, designed in 1980, which is a playful reminder of the children's game of reflecting sunlight with a mirror. Vico Magistretti is the creative mind behind the simple elegance of the Carimate Chair. And Franco Albini did not only give the now-iconic Albini Desk his name, but he also shaped the underground of Milan by designing numerous subway stations. All three are among the aesthetical visionaries who made Milan the capital of design. Today, their studios are the *Fondazione Franco Albini*, the *Fondazione Achille Castiglioni*, and the *Studio Museum Vico Magistretti* (pictured)— all small spaces run by foundations or their families, making it possible to take a closer look at their ideas, prototypes and work. Discover how the concept for the legendary Flos Arco floor lamp came to be, or where the design for the department store La Rinascente was developed. Be sure to make a reservation for a visit—if you are lucky, you will have their sons or nephews as guides. They might even share private tales about the lives and working methods of these design pioneers.

• Various locations, see Index p.65

Global Styles

Housed in a former 18th century convent in the beautiful 5 Vie neighbourhood, *Wait and See* fuses colourful dresses with home accessories, shoes and jewellery. The atmosphere is reminiscent of the charming mess you might find at a flea market. Uberta Zambeletti, the owner of the store, was a design consultant for Missoni and Etro. Rooted in her interest and passion for travel, her mix of clothing styles caters to women from all over the world: from California and France to Finland and Peru. Enjoy a cup of coffee, maybe sipped from a "La Vita è Bella" mug, and spend a moment meditating on the chalk phrases scrawled upon the sidewalk in front of the shop— the staff writes a new motto every day.
• Wait and See, Centro, waitandsee.it

Food | Taste of the Town

Locals joke that you need to take a day off if you're going to eat at *Nuovo Macello*. Perfect, then, if you don't have to work. After a short journey out of the city centre, the trattoria-style ambiance welcomes you with an authentic feeling of heritage. But just wait for the food: the dishes playfully combine rustic and chichi. The Tokyo beef tartar is a classic, the thick-cut veal cutlet served medium is a must, and the gelato al Gorgonzola will make you want to applaud—at least on the inside.
• Trattoria del Nuovo Macello, Vittoria, trattoriadelnuovomacello.it

Outdoors Club Tropicana

As the summer sun thumps down on Milan beat the city heat with a touch of northern cool. *Ceresio 7* is a retro restaurant and cocktail bar boasting a fashionable crowd and two swimming pools. The Fascist-era building was redone by Dimore Studio for the fashion label DSquared—credentials to be appreciated in its impeccable design. On a hot night it's just the place to turn up around 7pm for an aperitivo in the glow of the sunset over the Milanese skyline.
• Ceresio 7, Garibaldi, ceresio7.com

Culture Flamingo Road

Quadrilatero del Silenzio is a historic district famous for its beautiful villas and hidden gardens. Just a few steps away from Villa Invernizzi, where the back garden houses a flamingo colony, *Villa Necchi Campiglio* exhibits its original interiors, telling the story of the important Lombard family, Necchi-Campiglio. The height of bourgeois elegance, the villa was built by the most in vogue architect of the 1930s, Piero Portaluppi. The entire house is open to the public and has a café inside that serves lunch.
• Villa Necchi Campiglio, Porta Venezia, casemuseomilano.it

Pierpaolo Ferrari
He is a photographer, publisher,
creative director and driving force in
the world of art and fashion. In 2010,
he teamed up with Italian artist
Maurizio Catellan to create "Toiletpaper",
an image-based magazine known
for both conforming to standards and
challenging them. Pictures featured
in the publication reveal not only the
stories of the subjects in focus, but also
the thoughts and ideas those subjects
trigger. Similarly wayward is Ferrari's
general approach to his work—nothing
is as expected. And yet, sometimes it is

Pierpaolo Ferrari, Artist/Publisher

Vantage Point

In city where the streets are paved with fashion designs and the calendar is awash with vernissages, the upcoming crowd is as important as the established brands. Pierpaolo Ferrari is the embodiment of Milan's respect for tradition and curiosity for new talent, and his vision of the Lombard capital is a collision of mainstream and eclectic

Post Design Gallery: a temple of postmodernist design

Are you originally from Milan?
Yes, I grew up in Milan and I believe it is a really cool city to live in. It isn't too big, compared with Paris or New York. You don't really need a car here, you can just take your bike and go everywhere. Milan is also a good base for work, thanks to the fashion industry. At the same time, the city has a lot of culture which is becoming more and more modern.

What other developments have you noticed?
The city has grown so much in the last few years since the investments for Expo Milan in 2015. The area I grew up in has radically changed. I like this and hope to be part of this renovation, but I have to confess, I also like my old Milan. If you take a walk at sunrise from

Piazza della Borsa to Piazza Duomo you will see the city as it was when I was a kid.

In one sentence, how would you describe Milan?
Elegance, in which tradition and modernity meet.

Is the city a source of inspiration for "Toiletpaper"?
Everything that happens in "Toiletpaper" happens in Milan.

What inspires you most in the city?
The fog in the winter. I love it when it's so thick that you can't see further than your own nose.

You travel a lot. What is the first thing you do when you come back to the city?
I love coffee! The longer I stay

abroad, the more I miss my favourite café. It's *Trattoria Bolognese da Mauro*, a small and traditional bar.

Is there something missing in Milan?
I would like to see more bars and cafés with tables in the street, like in Paris.

Where in Milan do you live?
I live in Porta Venezia—my studio is in the same building as my apartment. This neighbourhood is the perfect slice of Milan. It's full of ethnic restaurants and excellent traditional cuisine, and there's a great mix of people living there. It's a real place with real people, so it's a very human neighbourhood. There is *Villa Necchi*, from the architect Portaluppi, our Italian Frank Lloyd Wright, and the museum *Casa Museo Boschi di Stefano*, with its collection of over 300 artworks, including works by Giorgio de Chirico, Mario Sironi and Giorgio Morandi.

Do you have a favourite street in this area?
Via Mozart. I love it for all the really amazing buildings you can discover while walking there.

What is currently the coolest, hippest place to be in Milan?
Lambrate is becoming one of the most interesting areas for art and new galleries.

Speaking of art, is there an image that best represents Milan in your view?
Leonardo da Vinci's "The Last Supper". This painting alone is a really good reason to visit Milan. You can see it at the Piazza Santa Maria delle Grazie.

What is Milan's art scene like now?
The art scene in Milan is difficult to describe. There are very few

independent galleries and no support at all from the institutions to establish a new, strong generation of artists. Milan concentrates on business and is a very fast city. The art world is more a game of fashion.

Are there any young Milanese artists you have your eye on?
Roberto Cuoghi, who lives and works in Milan.

What is your favourite gallery?
Le Dictateur and *Massimo De Carlo*. For opposite reasons, but I think they should do something together.

Are there any underground art venues that you would recommend visiting?
Le Dictateur gallery again, and also *Peep-Hole Gallery* and *Archivio Farini*.

If you had a day off in Milan, how would you spend it from morning to evening?
The best would be if I could spend it with my girlfriend. Breakfast at *Pasticceria Sissi* where I would spend an hour eating brioche filled with cheese and where I can read "Corriere della Sera", an Italian newspaper. Followed by a walk to the Duomo square to see an exhibition, then lunch at *Latteria Vegetariana*, where I would eat "misto forno"—don't forget the name of this dish, I highly recommend it. In the afternoon, gardening and happy hour at *Bar Basso*.

Where do you go to escape from the city?
If the weather is good, I go to the Trebbia River. It's 45 minutes away from Milan. You will find crystal clear water and canyons of beautiful rocks.

Antoniolo Boutique
Navigli

FRIP
Centro

Dimore Gallery
Centro

Jannelli e Volpi
Porta Venezia

Galleria Post Design
Centro

10 Corso Como
Garibaldi

Il Carpaccio
Porta Venezia

La Terza Carbonaia
Porta Venezia

Da Giannino
l'Angolo D'Abruzzo
Porta Venezia

La Piccola Ischia
Porta Venezia

Pasticceria del
Capitano Rosso
Porta Venezia

What is your favourite season in Milan?
From March to September, Milan is the best city in the world.

Milan has long been an established city in the fashion world. Do you think its importance is still justified today?
I think there are only two cities with the top elegance in the world, and those are Paris and Milan. This is simply a matter of fact.

Prada, Versace and Armani are some of the big brands that ensure Milan's reputation in the fashion world. Are there also new interesting designers and labels emerging?
Massimo Giorgetti from MSGM and Marcelo Burlon. These are two young and talented designers.

Is there a certain style of dress in Milan?
Yes, there is a classic Milanese style. It consists of the green Loden jacket, a double-breasted blazer and leather shoes that your grandfather would have worn.

Where do you go shopping for clothes?
Fratelli Rossetti for shoes. Suits and shirts at Prada. I don't do a lot of shopping.

Is there a store that offers upcoming designers?
Yes, *Antonioli Boutique* as well as *FRIP*.

And when it comes to other products, such as items for the home, where do you go?
I love design and I go crazy for any Fornasetti piece from Creazioni d'Interni. I just bought a table from the 1960s by Giampiero Romanò and I could buy everything from *Dimore Gallery*, order custom wallpapers from *Jannelli e Volpi* and

get a chair by Marco Zanini from *Galleria Post Design*.

What's your favourite book store?
10 Corso Como.

Now let's talk about Italy's famous cuisine. What is your favourite traditional dish?
Polenta, as well as "ossobuco alla milanese", "risotto alla milanese" and "cotoletta alla milanese" are my favourite dishes. They are all yellow—the colour of the sun.

Where in Milan do you get these dishes?
Il Carpaccio, La Terza Carbonaia, and *Giannino l'Angolo D'Abruzzo.*

And where would you get the best pizza?
No doubt about that: *La Piccola Ischia.*

And pasta?
Giannino l'Angolo D'Abruzzo. You will get the best carbonara in town there.

And ice cream?
At *Capitano Rosso*. I love lemon ice cream.

And what is the best pasticceria in Milan?
The best for me is Capitano Rosso. They even do the catering when we're on the set for "Toiletpaper" magazine.

16

Above: The Dimore Gallery features objects from the past and the present
Below: The legendary 10 Corso Como features a bookshop, an art gallery, a café and a clothing store

Upper East Side

A decade ago, this area was a shady place. Today the streets around Porta Venezia are rich with culture and taste, mixing the best of the old with new influences from all over the world

Night | **So Wrong it's Right**

Decades ago *Bar Basso* became the first-ever Milanese joint to introduce the "aperitif" to every-day people. It remains a not-to-be-missed meeting place, famed for its signature cocktail: the Negroni Sbagliato ("wrong negroni"), invented here and served on ice in huge glasses like movie props. During Milan Salone del Mobile weeks it's become the place for international designers and journalists to gather. But be warned: asking for an aperitivo is not the done thing during these mega-parties. Instead, drink cocktails at the counter with nuts, olives and chips—as it's been done for years.
• Bar Basso, Via Plinio 39, Porta Venezia, barbasso.com

House of Arts

Designed by Ignazio Gardella, the *PAC* pavillion opened way back in 1947 next to the impressive Galleria D'Arte Moderna Milano. But it's since 1979 that the Padiglione d'Arte Contemporanea has focussed all its exhibitions on contemporary art. The shows held in in its 1,200-square-metre space have represented an eclectic approach: from solo shows for photographers like Silvio Wolf and performances by Vanessa Beecroft, to themes such as the crosspoint between modern art and cinema. On Thursdays, admission is half price and the museum stays open until 10:30pm for some late contemplation.
• PAC, Via Palestro 14, Porta Venezia, pacmilano.it

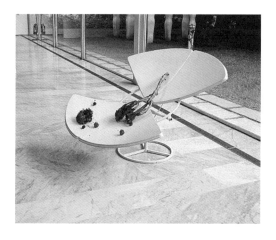

Food   Aristocratic Tastes

In comparison to the restaurant Giacomo whose focus is on fish, the sibling *Giacomo Bistrot* has a simpler and faster kitchen, majoring mostly in meat. But like a Parisian bistro, it serves also oysters or truffles—when in season—together with champagne and fine wines. Here, tables are set close together in the French style, while shelves loaded with leather-bound volumes evoke the British ambience of a traditional bookshop. Continuous service is offered from lunch straight through to 2am, making it the perfect place for a late night dinner.
• Giacomo Bistrot, Via Pasquale Sottocorno 6, Porta Venezia, giacomobistrot.com

Food · Shop   Calm and Cosy

Paola and Katia manage the tiny space of *Pause* with charm and flair to create a relaxed, living-room atmosphere that's both chic yet informal. The environment is micro but delicious—the room is just big enough for a small counter, a few tables and some booths where vintage clothing and accessories are exhibited. Everything here is for sale, and the owners also organise photo exhibitions and events. Pause is good for a break any time of day—starting from breakfast at 8am and ending with happy hour in the evening.
• Pause, Via Federico Ozanam 7, Porta Venezia, pausemilano.com

More than Meat

Though the name of *Non Solo Lesso* tells you it doesn't *only* serve boiled meat, it still does a mean version of the traditional "lesso" stew. But the menu is also awash with other Lombard and Piedmontese classics, including "Brasato al Chianti", a tender piece of beef braised for three days in red wine. With the kitchen family run for three generations, the atmosphere is much like an Italian home—with guests of all ages eating and drinking together at the large wooden table. And the kitchen remains popular with Milanese diners, especially when the temperature starts to drop.
• Non Solo Lesso, Via Broggi 13, Porta Venezia, nonsololesso.it

Shop **From Albini to Zanuso**

Claudio Loria is a stylish Milanese gentleman with a taste for fine furniture and art. With his team of interior designers he has worked for brands like Louis Vuitton, Trussardi and MTV. In Porta Venezia, his roomy space holds a curated collection including rare pieces from Italian icons such as Joe Colombo and Ettore Sottsass, as well as from lesser-known designers. Since 2012 Claudio has also produced his own small collection of furniture. During the Design Week, *L'Eclettico* is the spot to meet in town and has become one of the most sought-after exhibition spaces.
• L'Eclettico, Via San Gregorio 39, Porta Venezia, leclettico.it

Night **Speakeasy**

Few are the initiated who know of this Milanese bar, inspired by the US era of Prohibition. Not only is the location disguised and inconspicuous, but only an invitation will grant you access through the small hidden back door. Once inside *Club1930*, you will find a living-room atmosphere with cosy corners, good music and excellent cocktails. Naturally we can't reveal the location on these pages: those keen enough will have to cross the city to the MAG Café at Ripa di Porta Ticinese where you can get your hands on an invite.
• Club1930, by appointment only

Food · Night | Il Gusto della Tradizione

The neighbourhood of Porta Venezia lends itself to a nostalgic voyage. Those after an original Italian 1960s atmosphere—with shades of a Luchino Visconti movie—should descend on *Bar Picchio*. The simple neighbourhood bar has a friendly, familiar atmosphere and local food, freshly made by the owners. Delicious at any time—but it's at its best during aperitivo hour. Go there often enough and you might gain inclusion in the photo gallery of loyal patrons. Not too far away is *Polpetta DOC* (pictured), a traditional wine bar and meeting place for every generation. This family-run establishment is pleasant and inviting, with wooden chairs, exposed red-brick walls and owners attentive towards every customer. Be sure to try their home-made meatballs. Try not to get any on your shirt though, as a 1920s-style ballroom awaits you in *Sala Venezia*. Follow the "Animazione" signs to this hidden spot, thick with a genuine, vintage atmosphere. In years past, the dance hall was frequented by an audience aged 60 and upward. But now, it's grown in popularity with a younger crowd, thanks especially to its infamous Sunday evening "Boogie Night". With affordable food and drinks pulling in the punters, make sure you reserve in advance to get into this popular spot.

• Porta Venezia, various locations,
see Index p.65

Marco Maturo and Alessio Roscini
They are the founders and designers
of Studio Klass, an Italian industrial
design agency based in Milan. From
toothbrush holders to lamps, tables
and clocks, Maturo and Roscini trans-
form utilitarian products into aestheti-
cally pleasing objects. In doing so,
they prove that Italy's, and especially
Milan's, reputation for interior and
product design is well founded

Marco Maturo & Alessio Roscini, Product Designers

New Traditions

From music, art, food and architecture to fashion and furniture design,
Italians have excelled throughout history in various disciplines. But is
it possible to put a contemporary spin on centuries of artisanal tradition
without succumbing to modern factory processes? Marco Maturo and
Alessio Roscini show that contemporary designers can borrow from
history while remaining independent

You travel a lot due to your job and probably meet people who have never been to Milan. How would you describe the city to them?

Marco: I list three peculiarities. First, the aperitivo. It's a nice moment to enjoy a drink with your friends but it is also a good opportunity to meet people and share ideas. I think a lot of business comes out of aperitivo time. After work people are more relaxed and more open to new challenges. Secondly, there are well-dressed people all over the city. And thirdly, Milan is not a big city, but you will never stop discovering it. After ten years living here, I still find new spots and new places.

Alessio: I totally agree. Especially in regard to working in Milan. The city has a deep work ethic, with respectful people working alongside each other in a fair way.

Is Milan still a source of inspiration?

Marco: I think the most interesting sources of inspiration for designers are art and fashion design. You can learn a lot from those fields and Milan, especially, offers so much in these two disciplines. The city is full of small art galleries and boutiques.

Alessio: For me Milan is not necessarily the most influential source of creative inspiration for our designs. But the city is the place to be in Italy because it's the centre. All companies have their showrooms here and there are a lot of design events—so it is the perfect meeting point.

What inspires you?

Alessio: We've had the chance to work with companies that have decades of experience in a particular business and it is this heritage that is a strong source of inspiration for me.

Marco: Milan is often described as the "city of appearances" and at times this is probably true—particularly if you don't try to get to the essence of the city. The extraordinary thing is there are hundreds of amazing spots around the city not easily found unless you are willing to walk for hours in the right neighbourhoods, such as Porta Venezia. Sometimes we like to get out of the studio to enjoy a walk around this area, looking at the breathtaking buildings of the late 18th and early 19th centuries that are not mentioned in any city guides. They don't scream their beauty; they just exist and people live in them.

Where is your studio located?

Alessio: Our studio is on Via San Gregorio. In the 1980s this was the main street of a neighbourhood full of fabric shops. Nowadays, it's full of offices, so it's very lively during working hours. In my opinion, it's difficult to talk about the identities of Milan's neighbourhoods. The atmosphere dominating two or three streets can be totally different just around the corner.

Marco: That's true, and of course, the atmosphere changes with time. The area where our studio is located is named Porta Venezia. Until a few years ago, the neighbourhood was renowned for its underground scene and was seen as a dangerous area. Apart from a few streets that you still shouldn't walk by after 5pm, the situation has changed over the last six or seven years. Today the neighborhood is a melting pot of different cultures and nationalities. It's full of hipsters, gay-friendly clubs and bars, ethnic restaurants and very nice places for breakfast. At the moment, it's definitely the most multicultural area of the city.

"I Sette Palazzi Celesti" ("The Seven Celestial Palaces")—Anselm Kiefer's installation at the Fondazione HangarBicocca

morning. The atmosphere makes you feel at home. The guys working always have a smile on their faces and you can even bring your laptop. Most importantly, the food is great. It's freshly made every day. I strongly recommend visiting this place.

Business dinner?
    Alessio: *Ratanà*. It's a restaurant that serves Milanese food inside a great location that was originally part of a train station. You will definitely need a reservation if you want to go here for dinner.

And private?
    Marco: *Non Solo Lesso*. The restaurant has just five or six tables, so you need to make a reservation. The atmosphere is very friendly, like being at home with your relatives while you enjoy good original food from Lombardia, the Milanese region, and Piemonte, the region of Torino.
    Alessio: *Ta-Hua*, a traditional modern Hong Kong restaurant just near my home.

As designers, you probably see details in this city which others probably wouldn't even notice. What do you consider the most beautiful, intriguing spot in Milan?
    Marco: The *Palazzo Berri-Mere-galli*. It's a weird, austere building from the first half of the 19th century. From the outside, it's full of sculptures, mosaics and paint-ings. This one building mirrors all the architectural styles of the last century, from Romanesque to Liberty and from Gothic to the Renaissance period. They are all well mixed together. It seems like the architect was a bit uncertain how he should design the building. It's crazy! I like it.
    Alessio: What I like a lot are the big sliding windows of the

L'Antro della Sibilla
Porta Venezia

Pavè
Porta Venezia

Ratanà
Isola

Non Solo Lesso
Porta Venezia

Ta-Hua
Isola

Palazzo
Berri-Meregalli
Centro

Italians love their midday break. What do you do for lunch?
    Alessio: When you live in a neighbourhood, and spend so many hours a day in it, at some point you become part of it. We are friends with many bar and restaurant owners. Sometimes we go for lunch at their places just to enjoy a familiar mood and to chat and relax for an hour. Most often, we will end up having lunch at *L'Antro della Sibilla*, a restaurant founded by two friendly guys from Naples.

And for lunch with clients?
    Marco: *Pavè*. It's a restaurant very close to our studio. I have breakfast there almost every

The design of good furniture is an art—so is it presented at the Nilufar Gallery

residence-houses on Via Agostino Bertani 10 designed by Giulio Minoletti in 1965–70. Each mini-apartment is organised in such a way as to place the relationship with the green of Sempione Park in the forefront. From the street side you can only see a geometric pattern of windows and pillars.

And which place in Milan is the most beautifully furnished?
Marco: I'm so fascinated by the old design brand *Azucena* and one of its founders, Luigi Caccia Dominioni. The store is located in the city centre and is very small and not easy to find. In my opinion, it's one of the most beautiful places in Milan in regards to interior design.

Alessio: If I think about an ideal interior, I believe the hardest to match is the house of *Villa Necchi Campiglio*. Its 1930s–1940s interior was first designed by Piero Portaluppi and then by Tomaso Buzzi.

What about a museum or gallery that focusses on interiors?
Marco: *Nilufar Gallery*.
Alessio: Oh yes, that's very nice.
Marco: Plus *Dilmos Gallery*.
Alessio: And *Galleria Luisa delle Piane*.

What is the most inspiring furniture store in Milan?
Marco: *Understate*. The name says it all. They sell unique pieces and products from design brands. If you are looking for inspiration for your home, go there and ask the owner for help.

Alessio: You definitely shouldn't miss the one-brand showrooms of the most famous design companies such as Poliform, Herman Miller, DePadova, Unifor, Cassina and Zanotta.

And when it comes to vintage furniture?
Alessio: *Roberta E Basta*. They have a great selection of extremely rare and unique pieces of Italian and French Art Deco.
Marco: *L'Eclettico*. It's more of a design gallery than a design shop, but the furniture selection is accurate and you can find unique vintage pieces from around the world.

Are there also nice flea markets?
Marco: *Al Mercatino Tra Noi e Voi* is nice. It's a crammed family-run market not far from the Central Station. Go and have a look. You will find everything from cheap plastic accessories to vintage original Artemide or Flos lamps.
Alessio: I like going to the flea market at Piazzale Cuoco on Sunday mornings. It's the only one that has not become posh, but keeps with the original rude style.

When it comes to product design, is there a store in Milan that sells a great selection of well designed products?
Marco: Oh yes, *Spazio Rossana Orlandi*. The selection is made by the eponymous and internationally renowned Rossana Orlandi. It's an incredible place. You can go and after you have visited the gallery you can enjoy the shop where you will find everything from handmade plates, glasses, chairs, lamps, accessories, etc.
Alessio: My favourite is *Arform*, a store specialising in home and kitchen products. They offer a selection of niche brands and

high-quality products, both for design and materials.

Where do you go to see art exhibitions?
Alessio: I often visit contemporary art galleries. I suggest going to *Cardi Black Box* gallery, *Massimo De Carlo*, *Monica De Cardenas* and *Jerome Zodo*.
Marco: I suggest *HangarBicocca*. It's a contemporary art foundation, probably the best one in the city. There is also *Galleria Giò Marconi*, an art gallery in the Porta Venezia area and *Pinacoteca di Brera*. I like to visit it on Saturdays. You'll find masterpieces from Renaissance Masters like Piero della Francesca and Caravaggio there.

Is there a space that focusses on exhibiting architecture?
Alessio: Next to Spazio, *FMG per l'Architettura*. It also hosts very interesting exhibitions on architecture.
Marco: The *Triennale di Milano*. It's probably the most important design and architecture museum in Italy.

Daily Dose
Invisible Design in the Public Space
Stefano Mirti

We all know Milan is the capital of design. Is it true? Is it not true? For the benefit of our short piece, let's assume that Milan is one of the global capitals of design. Design is a synonym for Milan, with fashion being a second and football a third. But, for the time being, let's focus on design. Milan and design. There is Salone del Mobile, the Fuori Salone, the Italian tradition, the masters, the companies, and the products; a lot of different ingredients all relating to design. Yes, of course we can agree that Milan is the capital of design.

Design is everywhere. As Italians, we love and ride Vespas, we make our coffee in the morning with a Bialetti Moka, we like to furnish our homes with timeless masterpieces—just because we like them, not because they are masterpieces. And there's one more thing...

In a city like Milan the most beautiful and sophisticated designs are often found in public spaces—so blatantly obvious that they become invisible. If you want to see and enjoy some of the finest pieces of the Italian design tradition then the only thing you need to do is walk around. You don't need to shop or buy, just stroll around and you are in history. The designs are so incredible that they become invisible—just by being there, for everyone to see and use.

Here are two examples that explain this idea:

You arrived at Malpensa airport. Here there are so many complexities to take in, that few visitors spend the time enjoying one of Ettore Sottsass' most incredible projects. To enter an extravagant house and spot Sottsass' furniture is quite exciting, but the concept of having the city's main airport designed by Mister Memphis himself is one step beyond. So beyond, that 99% of stressed travelers don't even notice it. Malpensa Terminal 1, not to be confused with the new wings, was designed by the Sottsass Associati at the peak of their influence in the year 2000. To have an airport designed by a Norman Foster or Renzo Piano using high-tech vocabulary would be an obvious choice. To have it done in post-modern style—well that's something you won't find anywhere else in the world.

If you enjoy postmodern design, and airports, then after Malpensa you must go to Linate. Here you'll find some of the impressive Aldo Rossi's work in the airport extension (1991/1993). Although less powerful than Malpensa, you can still take in a full view from the landing strips.

Another example? Take the subway in either direction: "linea rossa" (red line) or "linea verde" (green line). If Ettore Sottsass was the king of postmodernism, Franco Albini was the knight of the modernist Italian style. In one of the stations, take a break and stop for a moment. Spend ten minutes observing the details: handrails, colour palettes, surfaces, and various objects. These all lend to one of the finest examples of the Italian 1960s. A whole universe built between 1962 and 1969. A collaboration between the architects Franco Albini and Franca Helg, and the visual identity and graphic designs of Bob Noorda. Isn't it beautiful? Wasn't it worth the stop? How come you never noticed it before? Franco Albini is one of our favourite architects and designers. The Metropolitana

Linea Rossa designed by Franco Albini, a fine example of 1960s Italian design

is one of his best works: a woman, more than 50 years old, and still quite timeless. The older she gets, the more fascinating she becomes (indeed, not an easy task).

Is the Albini modern language not strong enough for you? Do you want more? Do you like things hardcore? Then take the "passante" urban train and make sure you get off at Rogoredo or Certosa station. The architect was Angelo Mangiarotti in the year 1982. A lot of the stations along the passante were designed by him: Bovisa, Repubblica, Porta Venezia. But Rogoredo and Certosa are the most impressive. It is difficult to separate engineering from architecture from product design, making this whole system quite a feat. The Rho-Pero station (Fs), from 2006, is one of his latest works.

Of course we could give you many other examples. Think for instance of Stazione Centrale; designed by Ulisse Stacchini and opened in 1931. Its mesmerising architecture is impossible to link to any known style. It looks as though it's from some Mesopotamian kingdom, but we can't even be sure of that. Or, travelling back in a time machine, we could arrive at the original Navigli system developed by Leonardo da Vinci. If you weren't aware of this accomplishment by Leonardo, you can still see some of its fascinating leftovers in Via San Marco.

Of course the list could be longer, but this is a good start. The most impressive part of this whole story is that Milan has a sizable amount of "design for all". Design in public spaces, but oddly enough, design that is always related to some practical function. Italy is a country of theatre, of being constantly on stage—a country where form follows form. Palazzi, piazze and the rest. The Italian square, a place where you sit and lazily sip your aperitivo beneath a nice sunset; design for pleasure, leisure design. To this extent Milan is an exception. Milan is undoubtedly unItalian, with a DNA that has function at its core. You can find design in anything: a train station, an airport, a subway infrastructure or a gas station. Of course, in Milan you'll find great palazzi and a huge amount of things constructed with the "bella figura" in mind, but in Milan there is that something else, something more, something beyond. Places, objects and systems where function is so relevant that it eats at form to become pure meaning.

Before we forget, if you like the "gas station" theme, please go to Piazzale Accursio where you'll find a mesmerising jewel designed by Mario Bacciocchi (1951/1953, originally for Agip).

It is design of the finest kind and since its primary goal is function we generally don't pay enough attention to it. Occasionally we'll notice it when it gets old, like the yellow cars running on the tramway network. Their official name is ATM Class 1500, a.k.a. Type 1928; 1928 because they started their honoured career in that same year. They are still running now.

Stefano Mirti is an architect, designer, teacher and founder of IdLab, Milan. He teaches at Milan's Bocconi business school, and is head of the relational design on-line/off-line master's at Abadir, Fine Arts Academy Catania. For many years he has been working on new forms of teaching, including Whoami, Design 101, Architecture 101 and several other projects

Daniela Aciu, Model
Alta Moda

Daniela Aciu
has been modelling in Milan
for the past two years. She
can be seen on runways
throughout fashion week,
working for well established
brands such as Armani
and Vionnet

Milan remains widely regarded as the capital of fashion, and its clothing industry employs an international crowd of designers, models and journalists to fuel the global demand for couture. Daniela takes us through her city; letting us in on where to find the best brands, the finest aperitivo and her best place to escape it all

How long have you been living in Milan?

I came to Milan from Transylvania, Romania, two years ago and I've never left since. Most of my model colleagues are based in New York and London and are quite surprised with my decision to settle here. They think it's a slow city, but that's exactly why I like it. This is one of the rare cities which can be calm and has something happening every single night, especially aperitivo, which I still don't understand but I enjoy!

What are your recommendations for aperitivo?

The rooftop of the Dsquared store has a great bar and restaurant called *Ceresio 7*, where they serve aperitivo in a nice environment.

What neighbourhood of Milan do you call home?

I live in Corso Como, close to Garibaldi station and very close to Chinatown. I love it here! On my street I have a small supermarket, a shoe maker, and a vegetable shop. It's like a little village.

What is the fashion scene like in Milan?

Milan is still the capital of fashion. I believe it is the city where most designers reside, although most of their clients are located outside of Italy.

Are there any younger designers?

Yes! I really like what CO|TE is doing at the moment. What's interesting in this city is how the older generation is supporting the younger one. "Vogue Italia" makes a real effort to promote young designers from within the city by covering the new generation. Also the older designers such as *Armani*, who owns a theatre in Milan and offers his space to young designers to produce their shows.

Compared to other cities, such as Paris, New York and London, what is special about Milan?

Because of my height I do a lot of runway shows and so I follow the circuit to New York, London, Milan and Paris. There is no alta moda (haute couture) in Milan—that's reserved for Paris. Milan is known for prêt-à-porter (ready-to-wear).

What brands do you work for here?

I had the opportunity to watch Armani work for a year. He is still very involved with the brand, examining every little detail.

Any shops you recommend?

The *Armani* complex on Montenapoleone. What he has accomplished is quite impressive—the Armani Hotel on top, a shop, and restaurants at the bottom. The *Nobu* restaurant is excellent. Mr. Armani lives and works around the block. He can sometimes be found inspecting the availability of the wines in the cellar. He's very involved with every aspect of the brand. *10 Corso Como* sells clothes from famous designers and also has a gallery, café and bookshop. *Excelsior* in Duomo is a multi-level centre that boasts minimal design and stocks the top brands. It also has a great food market. And *Nonostantemaras* is the showroom of the iconic designer Antonio Marras.

Where is your secret place to relax, away from the fashion world?

Bergamo, it's just outside the city. Bergamo Alta is on top of the hill, with fantastic views, restaurants and architecture.

Bellissima Padania

A showcase by Filippo Minelli

For some a dreary suburb, for others a sacred paradise. Padania is more than just a place: it's a state of mind. Traffic works, retail parks and blocky architecture await... Book your stay at visitpadania.com

Andrea Caputo, Architect
Urban Explorer

Andrea Caputo
He is an Italian architect who has gained international attention with his designs for the Carhartt WIP stores in Lisbon, Moscow and Seoul, and for the Retro Super Future flagship store in New York City. As an editor he has released several books on urban culture, shedding light on the global graffiti scene for example with "All City Writers". He has also launched a publication called "Public Domain", looking at the misappropriation of public and private spaces

Andrea sees his hometown through more than the eyes of an architect. His connections to the street art scene make him an attentive observer of urban lifestyle. He recommends Milan visitors free themselves from fixed tours—his own personal tips aside. It's the perfect city to discover on your own

Museo del
Novecento
Centro

How did you get into publishing and architecture?

During the mid-1990s I applied to a graphic design school in Milan. I was interested in established authors like Neville Brody, Bruce Mau, Ken Garland and other upcoming names from Europe like M/M Paris. Back then architecture was just a good way for me to escape obligatory military service. With a couple of exams per year it was possible to postpone the army. Graphic design school wasn't recognised as an "official" diploma, so architecture became my handicap, slowing down my other interests. I still remember Giovanni Denti, a great professor at Politecnico, obsessed with the essay "Ornament and Crime" by the Austrian architect Adolf Loos—my first architectural spark. Aside from that, I was still very involved in the European graffiti scene, taking part with actions and in fanzine publishing. Self-publishing, and mostly self-distribution, was the best way to travel and keep good connections with partners all over Europe and the US. I guess inter-railing kept youth culture networks together, giving the chance of sleeping on trains, visiting 10-20 cities per month and so on.

What distinguishes this city from others?

I don't see a big cultural or urban gap between Milan, Siena, Paris or Seoul. What distinguishes cities resides more in how you approach them. It is in the visitor's gaze. Milan is peculiar compared to other Italian cities. It seems to be permanently changing. It has its deep Italian roots but they are linked to a very international vision. These unique characteristics make it resemble other European and worldwide cities more than other Italian cities.

What are the best things in the city for you?

Currently the best thing is Lucifero, a serial graphic maniac who has taken over the whole public space of the city in the past few decades. You see his work everywhere and he says a lot about Milan—if you speak Italian! Then there is the *Museo del Novecento*, renewed by the architect Italo Rota. I would say every project by Italo Rota is worth a visit but this particular project is a personal favourite. Everyone should find out what the best thing in Milan is on their own. The city offers food for every taste. You can just walk through certain quarters and experience the life of the town.

Where can I discover some hidden architectural highlights?

Along Via Camillo e Otto Cima, in between the quarters Ortica and Segrate, there is a residential complex from the 1930s that was originally housing for railway workers. It's still impressive how these blocks remain in great condition today. In winter there's a sort of magic pervading the land between each condo; small green plots with English grass, fog and nothing else. Another place worth discovering is Vicolo delle Lavandaie, a narrow alley with a river in the middle. It's a place where women used to do laundry in centuries past, located just next to Navigli—a young area and the centre of nightlife. You can take beautiful walks there during the day. Another area that you would not expect to find in Milan is Villaggio dei Giornalisti, a district in the North with really elegant Liberty-style houses and strange buildings, such as igloo-houses. Here you can take nice architecturally stimulating walks and breathe the real life of Milan.

Talking about different areas, which are the juiciest city districts for you?

I think the Lambrate district is living a peculiar moment. It has become a district for the creative industry, with architectural offices and design galleries. A place where young people can develop their unconventional ideas, outside the main and academic streams. The area has moments of great success and visitor booms during Design Week, when people come for the numerous events that are organised. This is at the same time as the Salone del Mobile, the Milan furniture fair—which is always worth a visit.

Milan in a weekend—what are your recommendations?

Start with breakfast in Stazione Centrale at *Lux Bar Alemagna*. Then pay a visit to *One Off,* a lab for architectural models close to Stazione Garibaldi. For lunch I would recommend the Chinese *Trattoria Huacheng* in the Paolo Sarpi area. After that, pause for a coffee at *The Manhattan*. If you are interested in architecture, go for a short afternoon swim at *Piscina Cozzi*. It's a great way to see the amazing design of the space. You could then go for an aperitif at *Santeria Bar* in Via Ettore Palladini. If you like to sit back and observe life in the city, go to *Pizzeria Mundial* at Piazza Bottini. Since all of this is quite affordable, I suggest investing your daily budget at the *Osaka* restaurant in Corso Garibaldi. For the following day I recommend a lunch at *Osteria da Francesca*, Viale Argonne, where I am a local. These are all very personal recommendations and may be more of a list of intimate places, perhaps not interesting for tourist purposes. An alternative and more attractive plan could be breakfast at *Pavè* in Via

Casati near the Metro station Repubblica and a visit to *Hangar-Bicocca*, a permanent exhibition of contemporary art. You can follow that with a traditional Italian lunch at *Un Posto a Milano*, an agri-tourism restaurant in the centre near Porta Romana. After lunch you might be ready for some shopping in one of the diverse fashion streets of Milan, such as Corso Como or the historic Ticinese area. The *Deus Ex Machina* store is of interest for unique fashion finds.

What are your top three stores currently?

Moroni Gomma is a very nice lifestyle design store where you can be inspired and find things that you just can't get anywhere else. *Spazio Rossana Orlandi* at Via Bandello 14, has two floors and winds around a green courtyard. Here you can find vintage and contemporary furniture. Their gallery showcases unique pieces from young, upcoming designers from around the world. *Shame-Less* is great for designer vintage clothing, custom jewellery and various other rare finds.

If you take a rest, where do you feel most at peace?

In my office, but it's a private place. I would suggest *Upcycle*, an urban bike café. It's somewhere I can work, have meetings or just sit and enjoy a coffee in an unconventional place—an abandoned bike garage. Another option, for a sunny day, is Parco Sempione, the largest public park in Milan. You can walk or lie in the grass and rest. It also features the Castello Sforzesco from the 14th century. There is also the *Triennale di Milano*, a local art space built on the edge of park. During summer months the sculpture garden is open. The bar is also a nice place to hang out.

Un Posto a Milano is found in Cascina Cuccagna, a colonial house surrounded by a huge park

Triennale di Milano
Sempione

Coming back to your profession, if you were to predict Milan's architecture of tomorrow, what would it be?

My guess is it will remain very private. Major parts of the city—enormous city blocks if not entire neighbourhoods like Bicocca, Fiera—are developed independently from citizens, municipalities and public debate. They are developed architecture. New and random islands in the city. I don't see this as a 100-percent negative consequence. These varieties enrich the city and its inhabitants.

Furthermore, the expansion of the subway, with the conclusion of one line M5 and the construction of a new M4, presents an occasion to link districts distant from each other in geographical and architectural terms, and for suburbs to be requalified and redeveloped.

Back to the Future

The revitalisation that this once working-class neighbourhood has gone through divides the Milanese. Controversial skyscrapers tower over classic buildings; traditional trattorias feature alongside new cuisine

Culture | **Vertical Forest**

Monumental architecture and hyper-dense urban and industrial complexes shape the face of Milan. Recognising the human need for contact with nature, architect Stefano Boeri has attempted something radical and daring—combining modern architecture and metropolitan reforestation. The result? A sustainable residential high-rise in the heart of Milan's Porta Nuova neighbourhood, featuring 900 trees and over 2,000 plants. The building remains controversial with the Milanese today,

appearing in the skyline like an empty flowerpot. However, with time the architects hope the *Bosco Verticale* ("Vertical Forest") will pioneer sustainable living and be fundamental to the redevelopment of densely populated urban areas. It's already being taken as a shining example of a new movement in "Green Art" across the world—a way to bring back the forest and recolour our grey.
• Bosco Verticale, Via De Castillia, Isola, stefanoboeriarchitetti.net

Food | Vecchio-Nuovo

Combining the traditional with a modern twist is the idea behind the "Osteria" *Ex Mauri*. Inspired by the warm and friendly atmosphere of old Milanese taverns, this restaurant reinterprets classic dishes with a bit of creative cuisine. Even the ambience plays on the contrast between old and new, with the centre of the room overlooking an old open fireplace and a porthole in the floor that allows you to admire the ancient cellar. Ex Mauri is famous for its cod with polenta.
• Ex Mauri, Via Federico Confalonieri 5, Isola, exmauri.com

Food | Identità Milanese

Imagine yourself in a building that has miraculously survived a tumultuous urban makeover. It might be the different shades of white in contrast with each other that give the building a certain je ne sais quoi. Or perhaps its location, smack in the middle of Porta Nuova and a short walk from Garibaldi Station. Regardless, *Ratanà* is one of the most famous culinary addresses in Milan, thanks in part to Chef Cesare Battisti's exceptional risotto. It is Milanese cuisine at its finest and an oasis of culinary style in the midst of other modern "confusion" menus.
• Ratanà, Via Gaetano de Castillia 28, Isola, ratana.it

Shop | Discount Corner

Just a short walk from the legendary *10 Corso Como* boutique can be found its outlet. There is no sign, but once you've managed to find the entrance through a courtyard, you will be rewarded with small treasures at attractive prices. Clothing, shoes and accessories in the unmistakable style of the main store are on display at discounts of up to 50 percent, along with special discounts on small bags, jewellery and gadgets from five euros. Clearly worth that short walk.
• 10 Corso Como Outlet, Via Enrico Tazzoli 3, Isola, 10corsocomo.com

Shop **Taste the Taste**

Imagine entering your sophisticated, elegant friend's house and buying anything that takes your fancy. From the bed to a bookshelf—even the glass in which you're offered some wine. This is the experience at *Atelier Bellinzona*. In typical Italian style, proprietor Alberto welcomes you like one of his closest friends to what is his own small house and ex-laboratory, on the ground floor of a typical Milanese court building. From the moment you enter the feeling is of being in a special place, not only because of the eclectic originality, but thanks to the refined taste of everything surrounding you.
• Atelier Bellinzona, Via Carlo Farini 29, Isola, atelierbellinzona.com

Food **Family Business**

Trattoria da Tomaso is a real family-run restaurant where the son works the kitchen, the father serves tables and mom deals with the coffee and cash. The owner Paolo—not Tomaso as suggested on the sign—might seem a bit grumpy at times. But that's just because he is so busy. The restaurant is always full, mostly with workers, which makes it a bit tricky to find a place after 1pm. Best to come sooner—so you can try the full range of secondi too. With a true "trattoria" atmosphere, don't expect crystal glasses and silver cutlery. Even the prices seem to come from a time long past.
• Trattoria da Tomaso, Via Gaetano de Castillia 20, Isola

Night **The Song of Singing**

One evening in March 2003, one of Chick Corea's jazz standards flowed from the piano. This was the beginning of a ten-year love story between Milan and jazz music and, as time goes by, the two continue to be lovers. *Blue Note* has become one of the key venues in town to enjoy some sophisticated sounds in a fittingly smooth atmosphere. Select from over 200 cocktails while you listen to their exceptional jazz lineup, covering everything from pre-prohibition to the latest experiments.
• Blue Note, Via Pietro Borsieri 37, Isola, bluenotemilano.com

Motorcycle Diaries

Customised motorcycle culture has quickly become a trend from Venice Beach to Tokyo. And Italians always had a two-wheeled love affair going on, with iconic brands such as Ducati or Moto Guzzi playing an active role in their culture. Today, a molten pot of motorcycle madness can be found in an inner courtyard in Isola, at *Deus Ex Machina*. Peruse motorbikes, bicycles, surf gear, clothing— and even take a stop at a café. *Deus Ex Machina* translates as "God from the Machine"—a motto well suited for this temple of benzine. The clothing store features brands fit to equip the modern urban biker, like Carhartt and Barbour, and behind the store is a bike repair shop to get your new threads dirty. The location also offers a popular late night spot: one of the hot bars in Milan, where regulars sip cocktails in typical "Milano da bere" style. The drinks in themselves are a good reason to drop in and see what the crowd is up to. Ask for a Moscow Mule or the House Spritz, including secret ingredients. Could be engine oil—but whatever it is, it works.

• Deus Ex Machina, Via Thaon di Revel 3, Isola, deuscustoms.com

Riccardo Casiraghi & Stefano Paleari
Tutti Tasty

Riccardo Casiraghi & Stefano Paleari

They are the founders of Milan-based food blog "Gnam Box". Stefano's background is in graphic design while Riccardo is an interior designer—but it was their passion for food that brought them together. Since launching, their online business has gathered armies of loyal followers. The concept started with meeting creative people—by sharing a meal and getting to know them through cooking. They have published a seasonal recipe book, "In Food We Trust, Ricette di stagione", and collaborated with numerous food and fashion brands, such as Buitoni, Disaronno, Tommy Hilfiger and Missoni

Food lovers, food bloggers and online chefs, Stefano and Riccardo are a pair of flavour enthusiasts. Although they have done their fair share of exploration in foreign cuisine, there is no place like home for these Italians. They share with LOST iN their knowledge of their Milanese neighbourhood: from the best pizza to Michelin-star dishes

What makes Milan special for you?

Stefano: Milan is special for its mood and atmosphere. It's the kind of city that you will either love or hate on your first visit. You need to find your own personal Milan: your neighbourhood, your area, and your places. Sometimes it helps to live like a tourist. We're both from the countryside, near Milano, and moved here six years ago. We love to go around the city and discover new or old places, streets and shops. Milan is rich in streets with lovely backyards and old houses, especially in the city centre.

Riccardo: It's special because it's the city where we feel at home. But sometimes it can be hard to meet new people. This is one of the reasons we started inviting people to our apartment and letting them cook something for our website. Most are people we discovered online and are meeting for the first time when they knock on our door.

As food experts, which traditional dishes shouldn't be missed in Milan and where should they be eaten?

Stefano: Oh, good question! The traditional dishes you must eat in Milan are risotto, cotoletta, pizza, the Negroni Sbaglatio cocktail and gelato. You can find the best traditional cuisine in an old trattoria called *La Bettola di Piero*. At this restaurant you will have the perfect "Milanese" experience: red wine, risotto and traditional dishes. The street, Via Orti, is also very nice. You should stop for a drink at *Lacerba*, or a gourmet pizza at *Dry Milano*, in Via Solferino, where you can choose from many different pizzas with gourmet ingredients. This restaurant is relatively new to Milan—but very successful. For a typical cotoletta you have to go to *Antica Trattoria della Pesa*, a restaurant famous in Milan for this dish. For a cocktail we suggest *Bar Basso*, where they invented the Negroni Sbagliato. This bar is well known as a hot-spot for designers during Milan Design Week.

Riccardo: For good quality ice-cream, I suggest *Gelato Giusto*, Via San Gregorio 17. Here Vittoria, the owner, makes ice cream with seasonal products and only the freshest ingredients.

Where do you have your aperitivo before dinner?

Stefano: We're not very into aperitivo time and we don't like places with buffets or food on shelves. If you want to have a drink before dinner we suggest Dry Milano, the cocktail bar and pizzeria that we mentioned earlier. This place is really beautiful and you can have a gourmet pizza or focaccia with your cocktail. You must try their "focaccia con vitello tonnato". Guglielmo Miriello, the bartender at Dry, is one of the most famous bartenders in Italy and you can ask him to make the perfect cocktail for you. Another place is *Taglio*, in the Navigli area, here you can find an excellent selection of fine wines. Order a "Tagliere" with Italian cheese and salami—it's classic and delicious. Another great choice in the Navigli area is *Mag Cafè,* where you can really breathe in the international atmosphere and meet some nice people.

Where do you go after a nice dinner on the weekend to enjoy a drink and maybe some dancing?

Stefano: You can go to *Carlo e Camilla in Segheria*. The atmosphere there is amazing. It's in an old sawmill with a long table in the middle and beautiful chandeliers. The bar is really nice and you can try experimental cocktails served in amazing vintage glasses. For dancing we suggest you visit *Plastic*

Carlo e Camilla: cutting-edge design and a celebrity chef

Pavese and has a nice garden in the back. It's the perfect place to relax and rest your eyes and mind. If you want to try the Michelin-starred chef Davide Oldani, his restaurant is *D'O* and is in Cornaredo, 30km outside Milan.

Riccardo: Davide Oldani is famous for his "Cucina Pop" and as he says in his ten commandments that "every business needs to be profitable but prices should be fair". This restaurant is obviously famous for being top quality, but also for its lunch prices: from Monday to Friday you can taste the menu for less than 20 euros.

A new generation of Milan restaurants is rising, with young chefs and fresh concepts. Do you have three recommendations not to miss?

Stefano: For sure! You must try *Al Mercato Burger Bar* by Beniamino Nespor and Eugenio Roncoroni. Using the same kitchen from their first restaurant Al Mercato, they opened a little burger bar. These are the best burgers in town and you can taste the inspiration of these two chefs in them. Keep in mind, the place is very tiny so go early. Another good choice is *Fish Bar de Milan*, a concept by chef Eugenio Boer. This place serves a mix of traditional Italian fish recipes.

Riccardo: Another great concept is at *Pavè*, a bakery with a magical atmosphere and a "salotto" (parlour) too. Founded by three young friends, it's one of the most successful places in Milano. Everybody loves it!

What are the latest trends on the Milan food scene?

Stefano: The city is going through two different trends. One is connected to Michelin-star chefs and the other, which we love, is connected to simple and international cuisine. In the past few years

Club on Friday, Saturday or Sunday; every night has a different style of music and the people are always great. You could also try *Glitter Club* on Saturdays.

Riccardo: If you want to try something with a touch of the old, Italian style, then you must try the Balera at *Sala Venezia*. If you are in Milan in spring or summer, try the *Open Air Balera* in the Ortica area, just outside the city centre.

If the weather is nice, where do you sit outside to eat in Milan?

Stefano: If you are willing to go a little bit outside of the city, take a bike to *Erba Brusca*. This restaurant is on the Naviglio

Milan has seen a lot of cool new places founded by young and interesting people. We think it's the beginning of a new cuisine generation with European tastes; by people who travel a lot and have lots of fresh ideas and concepts. We believe in this new Milan for the everyday person, with the kind of places you can go to whenever you want.

Which markets do you like best?
Stefano: We suggest *Cascina Cuccagna*. It's open every Tuesday afternoon from 3:30pm to 8pm. Here you can find farm fresh products like vegetables, honey, and cheese. Another choice is *Popogusto*, a market organised by Radio Popolare. Their location for this year is in Arci Bellezza and is open every Saturday. They have everything from herbs, flowers, bread, fresh pasta, vegetables and more. For an organic shopping experience go to Centro Botanico where you'll find a selection of bio products and cosmetics. When we wake early on Saturday mornings we like to go to Mercato della Terra.
Riccardo: This market follows the guidelines of the organisation Slow Food, so you can talk directly with all the farmers and producers. Mercato della Terra is in Via Procaccini 4 at Fabbrica del Vapore.

Are there other shops that foodies shouldn't miss?
Stefano: If you love food, then you probably love cooking accessories as well. We suggest you to go to *Cargo/High-tech* near Piazza XXV Aprile where you can find lots of nice items for your kitchen. Near there is *Eataly Smerlando*, one of the markets in town to find the best Italian products. One of the most traditional food shops in Milan is *Peck*, near the Duomo.

This is the Italian temple of gastronomy. You must try everything!

In your opinion, what are the best cookbooks for Italian food?
Riccardo: Well first of all there's our book, "In Food We Trust". It focusses on learning how to eat in-season products. A cookbook that can be found in almost every kitchen in Italy is "Il cucchiaio d'argento", an encyclopedia for cooking with everything you need to know. We would also suggest "Street Food", a book by Beniamino Nespor and Eugenio Roncoroni from Al Mercato Burger Bar. The book is really interesting and also in English. The first part is rich in street food recipes and the second half is full of creative and sought-after recipes—a real mix of these two chefs.

Which is the best music to listen to when cooking an Italian dish at home?
Stefano: If you want to cook and listen to Italian music we suggest Mina or Lucio Battisti, two of the greatest artists from the Italian music scene of the past.

If you knew the world was going to stop turning tomorrow, where would you go for breakfast, lunch, and dinner?
Stefano: Lovely question. We would love to have breakfast at *Pavè*, a super burger lunch at Al Mercato Burger Bar, an aperitivo at Taglio and then a classic dinner at La Bettola di Piero.

Made in Milan

East Meets West

Produced by Seletti and CTRLZAK theses pieces juxtapose Chinese and European Bone China, displaying scenes and themes common to both cultures; the perfect way to confuse your grandmother next Christmas.
• Hybrid, Seletti, seletti.it

Leather Light

Founded in 2007, Wok defines itself as a conceptual store showcasing international designers and artists. Hand-picked by owners Frederica Zambon and Simona Citarella, each unique piece has undeniable style. This one-of-a-kind lamp has a sleek and modern design, making it a bright example of Milan's fashion-forward sensibilities.
• Rudi Rabitti Leather Table Lamp, Wok Store, wok-store.com

Seletti

...means umbrella and it's pretty likely that you will have to use one in Milan. This pop art print was contributed by TP Rossetti and the handle is wood. If someone asks why, just tell them "I saw it at MOMA."
• toiletpapermagazine.org

Books

A Private Venus
• Giorgio Scerbanenco, 1966

A doctor out of prison, Duca Lamberti is hired to straighten out a Milanese mogul's son. And that's when he gets sucked into the complex ring of prostitution and crime. From the father of Italian Noir.

Fiorucci: The Book
• Eve Babitz, Harlin Quist, 1980

A design book about the influential and inspiring brand world of Fiorucci. A true testament to the 1980s fashion scene. A rare find.

Due di Due
• Andrea di Carlo, 1989

De Carlo's love-hate relationship with his hometown, Milan, is detailed within his novels. The partially autobiographical "Due di Due" is about the friendship between the adventurous and radical Guido and the story's narrator—the more gentle and grounded Mario.

Movies

Milano Calibro 9
• Fernando Di Leo, 1972

The "Mano Armata" genre is characterised by brash, intricately plotted, ultra-violent gangster stories, told with attitude and style. Tarantino is known to have been influenced by these B movies.

La Vita Agra
• Carlo Lizzani, 1964

Based on one of the most significant contemporary Italian novels, "La Vita Agra" portrays a revolt against the cultural establishment of Milan. It's set in the 1960s in the aftermath of the economic miracle.

I am Love
• Luca Guadagnino, 2009

Set in Villa Necchi Campiglio, the movie, starring Tilda Swinton, is an ostentatious feast with a tremendous visual style. A tribute to the conflict between tradition and emotion.

Music

Ennio Morricone Go Jazz
• Jazz Workshop Orchestra & Enrico Intra, 2010

Pianist Enrico Intra has been a pioneer on the Italian jazz scene. In 1960 he founded "Intra's Derby Club" in Milan, where he played together with legends like Chet Baker and Gerry Mulligan. In his collaboration with Jazz Workshop Orchestra he performs classics by the Roman soundtrack maestro.

Mina Live '78
• Mina, 1978

Mina's music is like a good risotto: it nourishes the soul of everyone, from kids to grandparents. In 1978 the diva gave her last public concert, singing about joy, love and despair—and including an interpretation of Queen's "We are the Champions" as one of her goodbye tracks. Since then, she has released an album almost every year.

Leo Mas at Kundula
• Leo Mas, 2014

From Milan to Spain and back; Leo Marras has been one of the protagonists of the Ibiza club scene since the mid 1980s. He brought the Italian touch to Balearic Beats and the Summer of Love, and his latest releases, for labels like "Italian Records" and "Polluted", continue the vibe. His mix for Kundaluna is the perfect sound for a smooth night ride in an Alfa Romeo on Via Gallarate.
soundcloud.com/leo-mas

Straf Hotel

The Straf is a 19th-century palazzo next to the Duomo designed by Milanese architect, artist and designer Vincenzo de Cotiis. The hotel appears almost like an installation with its bare cement floors and stairs, scratched mirrors and rooms featuring oxidised copper. The guestrooms come in either a light or dark colour palette and all offer tactile pleasures in the form of fine textiles, decadent bathrooms and shiny surfaces. Besides the great aura of the hotel the Straf Bar is a spot to open up your inner sophisticate.

The Yard

The Yard is a concept guesthouse not far from the Duomo. Freely playing upon a timeless style, it offers a refined and relaxing atmosphere which uniting the spontaneous elegance of luxury and attention to comfort with the welcoming embrace of exclusive services. The Yard offers a selection of exclusive suites, ideal for short and long stays, in which guests can experience the exquisite pleasure of a friendly and informal environment, and recapture the warm feeling of home in the heart of Milan. The lobby is the real showpiece of The Yard and its philosophy; it is accessed through a door framed by steel flower boxes and delicate camellias.

Nhow Milan

Poised between classic and modern, trend and counter-trend, cosmopolitanism and the typical glamour of Milan: Nhow is imbued with originality and soaked through with contrasts. The former industrial building has been converted into an unconventional space that redefines the traditional concept of the hotel. A hub of unique and ever-changing experiences is there to be explored and experienced. And its location is right in the creative heart of Milan—a stone's throw from the most celebrated fashion and design showrooms.

Available from LOST iN

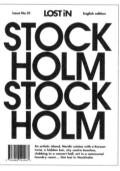

Next Issue: Ibiza

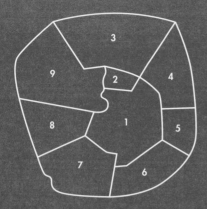

Districts

1/Centro

Al Mercatino Tra Noi e Voi
Via Giuseppe Marcora 8
+39 2 29 011 279
almercatinotranoievoi.com Ⓢ

Al Mercato Burger Bar
Via Sant'Eufemia 16
+39 2 87 237 167
al-mercato.it
→ p.55 Ⓕ

Armani
Via Alessandro Manzoni 31
+39 2 72 318 600
armani.com
→ p.33 Ⓢ Ⓕ

Azucena
Via Manzoni 23
+39 2 780 718
azucena.it
→ p.26 Ⓢ

Caffetteria DeCanto
Piazza della Scala 6
gallerieditalia.com Ⓕ

Camparino
Piazza del Duomo 21
+39 2 86 464 435
camparino.it

Dilmos Gallery
Piazza San Marco 1
+39 2 29 002 437
dilmos.com
→ p.26 ⓒ

Dimore Gallery
Via Solferino 11
+39 2 36 537 088
dimorestudio.eu
→ p.16 ⓒ

Dry Milano
Via Solferino 33
+39 2 63 793 414
drymilano.it
→ p.53 Ⓕ Ⓝ

Eataly Smerlando
Piazza XXV Aprile 10
+39 2 49 497 301
eataly.net
→ p.55 Ⓢ

Excelsior
Galleria del Corso 4
+39 2 76 307 301
excelsiormilano.com
→ p.33 Ⓕ

Fish Bar de Milan
Via Montebello 7
+39 2 62 087 748
fishbar.it
→ p.54 Ⓕ

FRIP
Corso di Porta Ticinese 16
+39 2 3315 800
frip.it → p.16 Ⓢ

Galleria Post Design
Via della Moscova 27
+39 2 6554 731
memphis-milano.com
→ p.16 ⓒ

Glitter Club
Via Filippo Turati 29
glitterclub.it
→ p.54 Ⓝ

Latteria Vegetariana
Via dell'Unione 6
+39 2 874 401
→ p.15 Ⓕ

Lux Bar Alemagna
Piazza Luigi Di Savoia 2
→ p.46 Ⓕ

Moroni Gomma
Corso Giacomo Matteotti 14
+39 2 796 220
moronigomma.it
→ p.46 Ⓢ

Museo del Novecento
Via Marconi 1
+39 2 88 444 061
museodelnovecento.org → p.45 ⓒ

Villa Necchi Campiglio
Via Mozart 14
+39 2 76 340 121
casemuseomilano.it
→ p.11, 26 ⓒ

Nilufar Gallery
Via della Spiga 32
+39 2 780 193
nilufar.com
→ p.26 ⓒ

Nobu
Via Gastone Pisoni 1
+39 2 6231 2645
noburestaurants.com
→ p.33 Ⓕ

Peck
Via Spadari 9
+39 2 8023 161
peck.it
→ p.55 Ⓕ

Pinacoteca di Brera
Via Brera 28
+39 2 72 263 264
brera.beniculturali.it
→ p.27 ⓒ

Roberta E Basta
Via Marco Formentini 4
+39 2 45 479 556
robertaebasta.com
→ p.27 Ⓢ

Studio Museo Vico Magistretti
Via Conservatorio 20
+39 2 76 002 964
vicomagistretti.it
→ p.9 ⓒ

Wait and See
Via Santa Marta 14
+39 2 72 080 195
waitandsee.it
→ p.10 Ⓢ

2/Garibaldi

Arform
Via della Moscova 22
+39 2 6551 448
arform.it
→ p.27 Ⓢ

Cardi Black Box
Corso di Porta Nuova 38
+39 2 45 478 189
cardiblackbox.com
→ p.27 ⓒ

Cargo/High-tech
Piazza XXV Aprile 12
+39 2 6241 101
cargomilano.it
→p.55 Ⓢ

Ceresio 7
Via Ceresio 7
+39 2 3103 9221
ceresio7.com
→p.11, 33 Ⓢ

**Antica Trattoria
della Pesa**
Viale Pasubio 10
+39 2 6555 741
anticatrattoriadella
pesa.com
→p.53 Ⓕ

Osaka
Corso Garibaldi 68
+39 2 29 060 678
milanoosaka.com
→p.46 Ⓕ

10 Corso Como Outlet
Via Enrico Tazzoli 3
+39 2 2901 5130
10corsocomo.com
→p.49 Ⓢ

The Manhattan
Via Alessandro
Volta 4
+39 2 43 111 679
→p.46 Ⓝ

Understate
Viale Francesco
Crispi 5b
+39 2 62 690 435
understate.it
→p.26 Ⓢ

3/Isola

10 Corso Como
Corso Como 10
+39 2 29 002 674
10corsocomo.com
→p.16, 33 Ⓢ

Atelier Bellinzona
Via Carlo Farini 29
+39 33 96 996 730
atelierbellinzona.com
→p.50 Ⓒ Ⓢ

Blue Note
Via Pietro Borsieri 37
+39 2 69 016 888
bluenotemilano.com
→p.50 Ⓒ Ⓝ

Deus Ex-Machina
Via Thaon di Revel 3
deuscustoms.com
→p.46, 51 Ⓕ Ⓝ Ⓢ

Ex Mauri
Via Federico
Confalonieri 5
+39 2 60 856 028
exmauri.com
→p.49 Ⓕ

Ratanà
Via Gaetano de
Castillia 28
+39 2 87 128 855
ratana.it
→p.25, 49 Ⓕ

Shame-Less
Via Porro
Lambertenghi 17
+39 2 1020 858
shameless-milano.
tumblr.com
→p.46 Ⓢ

Ta-Hua
Via Gustavo Fara 15
+39 2 66 987 042
tahua.it
→p.25 Ⓕ

Trattoria da Tomaso
Via Gaetano de
Castillia 20
+39 2 6688 023
trattoriadatomaso.it
→p.50 Ⓕ

4/Porta Venezia

Bar Basso
Via Plinio 39
+39 2 29 400 580
barbasso.com
→p.15, 18, 53 Ⓕ Ⓝ

Bar Picchio
Via Melzo 11
+39 2 29 531 433
n.e →p.21 Ⓕ Ⓝ

**Casa Museo Boschi
di Stefano**
Via Giorgio Jan 15
+39 2 74 281 000
fondazioneboschi
distefano.it
→p.15 Ⓒ

Cascina Cuccagna
Via Privata
Cuccagna 2
+39 2 5457 785
cuccagna.org
→p.54 Ⓢ Ⓞ

Club1930
→p.20 Ⓝ

**Da Giannino l'Angolo
D'Abruzzo**
Via Rosolino Pilo 20
+39 2 29 406 526
dagianninolangolo
dabruzzo.it
→p.16 Ⓕ

Galleria Giò Marconi
Via Alessandro
Tadino 15
+39 2 29 404 373
giomarconi.com
→p.27 Ⓒ

Gelato Giusto
Via San Gregorio 17
+39 2 29 510 284
gelatogiusto.it
→p.53 Ⓕ

Giacomo Bistrot
Via Pasquale
Sottocorno 6
+39 2 76 022 653
giacomobistrot.com
→p.19 Ⓝ

La Terza Carbonaia
Via degli Scipioni 3
+39 2 29 531 704
terzacarbonaia.it
→p.16 Ⓕ

Il Carpaccio
Via Lazzaro Palazzi 19
+39 2 29 405 982
→p.16 Ⓕ

Jannelli e Volpi
Via Melzo 7
+39 2 205 231
jannellievolpi.it
→p.16 Ⓕ

Jerome Zodo
Via Lambro 7
+39 2 20 241 935
jerome-zodo.com
→p.27 Ⓒ

L'Eclettico
Via San Gregorio 39
+39 2 67 079 142
leclettico.it
→p.20, 27 Ⓒ

L'Antro della Sibilla
Via San Gregorio 37
+39 2 67 481 054
antrodellasibilla.com
→p.25 Ⓕ

La Piccola Ischia
Via Giovanni Battista
Morgagni 7
+39 2 2047 613
piccolaischia.it Ⓕ

Monica De Cardenas
Via Francesco
Viganò 4
+39 2 29 010 068
monicadecardenas.
com →p.27 Ⓒ

Non solo lesso
Via Giuseppe
Broggi 13
+39 2 36 533 440
nonsololesso.it
→p.20, 25 Ⓕ

Osteria da Francesca
Viale Argonne 32
+39 2 730 608
dafrancesca.it
→p.46 Ⓕ

PAC
Via Palestro 14
+39 2 88 446 359
pacmilano.it
→p.19 Ⓒ

**Palazzo Berri-
Meregalli**
Via Cappuccini 8 Ⓞ

**Pasticceria del
Capitano Rosso**
Via Castel Morrone 35
+39 33 84 051 687
massimopica.com
→p.16 Ⓕ

Pause
Via Federico
Ozanam 7
+39 2 39 528 151
pausemilano.com
→p.19 Ⓢ

Pavè
Via Felice Casati 27
+39 2 94 392 259
pavemilano.com
→p.25, 46 Ⓕ

Piscina Cozzi
Viale Tunisia 35
+39 2 6599 703
→p.46 Ⓞ

Polpetta DOC
Via Bartolomeo
Eustachi 8
+39 2 29 517 983
→p.21 Ⓕ Ⓝ

Sala Venezia
via Alvise
Cadamosto 2a
+39 2 2043 765
→ p.21, 54 Ⓕ Ⓝ

Trattoria Bolognese
da Mauro
Via Elia
Lombardini 14
+39 2 8372 866
→ p.15 Ⓕ

Upcycle
Via A. M. Ampère 59
+39 2 83 428 268
upcyclecafe.it
→ p.46 Ⓕ

Le Dictateur
Via Nino Bixio 47
+39 2 88 007 310
ledictateur.com
→ p.15 Ⓒ

5/Vittoria

Pasticceria Sissi
Piazza Risorgimento 6
+39 2 76 014 664
→ p.15 Ⓕ

Plastic Club
Via Gargano 15
→ p.54 Ⓝ

Popogusto
Via Bellezza 16
radiopopolare.it
→ p.55 Ⓢ Ⓞ

Trattoria del Nuovo
Macello
Via C. Lombroso 20
+39 2 59 902 122
trattoriadelnuovoma
cello.it → p.10 Ⓕ

6/Vigentina

Giannasi 1967
Piazza Bruno Buozzi
+39 2 58 321 114
giannasi1967milano.
blogspot.de
→ p.8 Ⓕ

La Bettola di Piero
Via Orti 17
+39 2 55 184 947
→ p.53, 55 Ⓕ

Lacerba
Via Orti 4
+39 2 5455 475
lacerba.it
→ p.53 Ⓕ

Un Posto a Milano
Via Privata
Cuccagna 2
+39 2 5457 785
unpostoamilano.it
→ p.46 Ⓕ

7/Navigli

Antoniolo Boutique
Via Pasquale Paoli 1
+39 2 36 566 494
antonioli.eu
→ p.16 Ⓢ

FMG per l'Architettura
Via Ambrogio
da Fossano
Bergognone 27
+39 2 89 423 702
spaziofmg.com
→ p.27 Ⓒ

Mag Cafè
Ripa di Porta
Ticinese 43
+39 2 45 489 460
→ p.53 Ⓕ Ⓝ

Nonostante Marras
Via Cola di Rienzo 8
+39 2 76 280 991
nonostantemarras.it
→ p.8, 33 Ⓢ

Taglio
Via Vigevano 10
+39 2 36 534 294
taglio.me
→ p.53, 55 Ⓕ Ⓝ

8/Magenta

Mercato della Terra
Via Procaccini 4
Via Luigi Nono 7
slowFoodMilano.it
→ p.55 Ⓢ Ⓞ

Spazio Rossana
Orlandi
Via Matteo
Bandello 14–16
+39 2 4674 471
rossanaorlandi.com
→ p.27, 46 Ⓢ

9/Sempione

Archivio Farini
Via Procaccini 4
+39 2 45 471 153
viafarini.org
→ p.15 Ⓒ

Fondazione Achille
Castiglioni
Piazza Castello 27
+39 2 8053 606
achillecastiglioni.it
→ p.9 Ⓒ

Fondazione Franco
Albini
Via Telesio 13
+39 02 498 2378
fondazionefranco
albini.com → p.9

Galleria Luisa
delle Piane
Via Giusti 24
+39 2 3319 680
gallerialuisadellepi
ane.it → p.26 Ⓒ

One Off
Via Luigi Nono 7
+39 2 36 517 890
oneoff.it Ⓒ

Peep-Hole Gallery
Via Stilicone 10
+39 2 87 067 410
peep-hole.org
→ p.15 Ⓒ

Trattoria Huacheng
Via Giordano
Bruno 13
+39 2 3451 613
→ p.46 Ⓕ

Triennale di Milano
Viale Alemagna 6
+39 2 724 341
triennale.org
→ p.27, 46 Ⓝ Ⓞ

0/Outskirts

Open Air Balera
Via Giovanni Antonio
Amadeo 78
Ortica
+39 2 70 128 680
→ p.54 Ⓝ Ⓞ

Carlo e Camilla
in Segheria
Via Giuseppe
Media 24, Tibaldi
+39 2 8373 963
carloecamillainseghe
ria.it → p.53 Ⓕ Ⓝ

D'O
Via Magenta 18
+39 2 9362 209
Cornaredo
cucinapop.do
→ p.54 Ⓕ

Erba Brusca
Alzaia Naviglio
Pavese 286
+39 2 87 380 711
erbabrusca.it
→ p.54 Ⓕ Ⓞ

HangarBicocca
Via Chiese 2
Bicocca
+39 2 66 111 573
hangarbicocca.org
→ p.27, 46 Ⓒ

Massimo De Carlo.
Via Privata Giovanni
Ventura 5, Lambrate
+39 2 70 003 987
massimodecarlo.com
→ p.15 Ⓒ

Nonostantemarras
Via Cola di Rienzo 8
Tortona
+39 2 76 280 991
antoniomarras.it
→ p.8 Ⓢ

Pizzeria Mundial
Via Giovanni
Bottesini 3
Lambrate
+39 2 2665 154 Ⓕ
→ p.46

Santeria Bar
Via Privata Ettore
Paladini 8
+39 2 3679 8121
santeriamilano.it
→ p.46 Ⓝ

THE MYSTERIOUS MAN

By
PALOLO
ROVERSI

FROM THE ORIGINAL TITLE
"MAN OF MYSTERY"

BEST DETECTIVE   No. 4 · 25¢
Selection

Krista Bursey

The Mysterious Man

Paolo Roversi

The man pushes me, giving me an assassin's glance; a glance full of resentment that will either terrorise you or make you snap like a spring. He doesn't give me time to react, quickly disappearing off the train. I don't even stop to think, instinctively following him to settle the matter. That's how I roll. I have to decide quickly and I don't hesitate, rushing after him. I had to. Maybe he stole my wallet when he pushed me but right now I don't have time to check. I hurry, so as not to lose him, and a thought passes through my mind—the man has a familiar face but I didn't get a clear enough look at him to be sure.

I follow him up the stairs of the station, crossing piazza Gobetti and into via Porpora. I know this part of Milan well, it's Lambrate. A city inside the city. A lively area, where journalists, actors, writers, workers and real Milanese people live alongside immigrants and students. It is evening and the lights of the street lamps illuminate via Adelchi. I keep walking, ensuring to keep a distance from him. This area is always vibrant. It has changed a lot over the last few years. At the end of the fifties, during the economic boom, many large factories were built here. One stands out above the rest, the Innocenti which produced cars and scooters like the Lambretta, the historic rival of the Vespa. The Lambretta is a part of Milan, but also a part of the world's image of Italy. It was iconic in the American film "Roman Holiday". Today the Innocenti factory has closed down and the workshops have been converted into lofts, art galleries and trendy clubs.

The man has disappeared behind a wood-framed glass door. Above it there is a yellow sign, but I can't read it from where I'm standing. I stop and look around. I have the impression that I'm not alone, as though someone were following me. Is it possible? Yes. I realise it when, from the corner of my eye, I notice a man with a hoodie. He has suddenly appeared behind me with another man, a scarf covering his face. They stare at me insis-tently, coming towards me from the opposite side of the street.

Who are these two people? Maybe I should have let it go, but it's too late now. I'm in for a penny, in for a pound. I push the wooden door open and enter the club. There are a lot of people inside and in the crowd I lose sight of the man. He has disappeared, as if swallowed by the whirlpool of people. He reappears, only for an instant. Suddenly, everyone moves aside, leaving a huge empty space at the centre of the club where the man stands. He has a knife in his hand; a long, sharp blade. I am about to shout when the lights go out.

Complete blackout. Around me there is only darkness. I'm sweating, breathing with difficulty. I want to back away but someone grabs me from behind and I can't move.

The lights suddenly come back on and there's an explosion of voices and shouts. The knife plunges into an enormous cream cake.

"Happy Birthday!" everyone shouts.

The two strangers have removed their hoods and scarves revealing the faces of my friends, and the mysterious man is the patissier who lives on the floor below me. Even my wife is here, smiling like the Cheshire Cat in the corner of the room, complicit and cunning. I am sure that she is behind everything. I had forgotten it was my birthday today. The surprise worked perfectly, but I was almost scared to death.

Paolo Roversi is a crime fiction writer from Milan. He specialises in "Noir Metropolitano"

Illustration by Krista Bursey

ON THE ROAD

The App for the Discerning Traveller

Explore insider recommendations and create your personal itinerary with handpicked locations tailored to your desires. Our selection of experiences ranges from independent boutiques, galleries, neighborhood bars to brand new restaurants. Experience a new city from within.

LOST iN